True Riches

A Biblical Study of Esther

Wanda MacAvoy

True Riches
You may use brief quotations from this novel in reviews,
presentations, articles, and books. For all other uses,
please contact *Common Sense for Uncommon People*
wandamacavoy.com
Scripture quotations are from the King James Version
(KJV).
ISBN-13:
978-1495433078

ISBN-10:
1495433072

Table of Content

Whether therefore ye eat,
or drink,
or whatsoever ye do,
do all to the glory of God.
1 Corinthians 10:31

She had it all! She was the queen: a palace in which to live, the finest clothes, servants, and royal banquets—it was all hers! She even possessed a rare beauty! But her true riches lay within her heart and shone brighter than the jewels upon her head.

Do our lives, as God's chosen vessels, reflect what is inside; or do we need to take a step back and ask, "What is inside of me?" Esther was not only of Jewish descent, she was a child of God: Her faith projected forward to a coming Messiah.

Are you a Christian in name only, or does your faith in the living resurrected Son of God, Jesus Christ, make you a born-again child of God?

This devotional about Esther is for the true believer, but if you are not certain of your true identity, take a moment to review the following:

"And all things are of God,
who hath reconciled us to himself
by Jesus Christ,
and hath given to us
the ministry of reconciliation"
2 Corinthians 5:18

This may seem like a strange verse to begin a study of salvation, but truly that is what salvation is—reconciling a sinful self to the perfect holy God!

When we consider the word "reconcile," we often think of two people having a disagreement and settling that disagreement. Webster defines reconcile as:

5

1. to cause to be friendly or **harmonious** again
2. ADJUST : SETTLE *reconcile differences*
3. to bring to **submission** or **acceptance**

The greatest conflict we will ever face in our lives is our conflict with God. He is perfect and holy and cannot even look upon sin. That is why Jesus made the statement on the cross:

"... My God, my God, why hast thou forsaken me?"
Mark 15:34

I am so thankful, as a Christian, that I will never say those words, because my Father God promises that He will never leave me nor forsake me! (Heb. 13:5)

So how does a sinner reconcile himself to God? He can't apart from the way that God has made possible through His only Son, Jesus Christ. There is absolutely nothing we can do about our sin! So what can wash away my sin? The answer is given in the old hymn which says, "*Nothing but the blood of Jesus!*"

Why did God make the way impossible for man to achieve on his own? Man is a proud creature. Can you imagine the mess we would be in if man could work his way into heaven?

Sadly, many churches teach that doctrine, and many people are deceived into thinking that it is true.   Psalm 51:17 states that God requires *"a broken spirit: a broken and a contrite heart."* Simply put, God is looking for humility.   Again, man is a proud creature!   If he could do anything to earn salvation, he would not see his need for God.

Are you *reconciled* to God? Has there ever been a time when you:

- Realized that you are a sinner
- Understood that you need to be punished for your sin
- Realized that there is no remedy of your own to clear your guilty verdict, except the blood of Jesus Christ and His resurrection
- Prayed and received the gift of salvation

If you have **not** done this, I would urgently encourage you to do so! To stand before God and be condemned as guilty would be a horrible thing! To have to "pay" the punishment for our sins ourselves in hell is beyond my comprehension. It is an amazing reality that the only difference between eternal life in and eternal death in hell is one decision: Will I submit to God's simple plan of salvation, or will I continue to believe that I am good enough on my own!

The following is a simple prayer of salvation:

Dear Heavenly Father,

I understand that I am a sinner and that I deserve to be punished for my sins in hell. I know that Jesus died on the cross for ME, and I ask You to take away my sin and for Jesus to be my personal Savior. Thank You for the price You paid on the cross for my salvation! And thank You for Your power over death in raising Him from the dead!

In Jesus' Name. Amen

A simple prayer uttered in faith is the only way to heaven–to reconciliation to our God!

As Christian women, we have a calling to let our lights shine in this dark sin-cursed world. The times in which we live are filled with compromise and watered-down half-truths. Truly, we do not have to shine too brightly to be seen! We are faced with the challenge of standing firmly on the solid Rock of God's Word, presenting to a dying world the chilling truth that there is an eternal punishment awaiting all who reject God's call of repentance, and couching this sober message in the immeasurable love of God!

Can we find any help for living the light-filled life in the book of Esther? Consider her life: She was a foreign captive, living in a God-forsaken land. Many of her people had grown cold often melding into the foreign culture and accepting its blessings, while completely ignoring God's commands. Does that sound anything like the day in which we live? Esther proved the power of one, and so can we!

As we study the life of Esther, we need to look for God's applications for our lives. We do not study the Bible for the **heads** alone—but for our **hearts** and **hands** as well. Keep asking the question:

WHAT NEEDS TO CHANGE IN MY LIFE FOR ME TO BECOME MORE LIKE CHRIST?

That's a good lifelong habit which will help each one of us to accomplish the lifelong goal of Christ-likeness!

DATE	Major Events Concerning Esther
586BC	Jews exiled to Babylon
537BC	Exiles return to Jerusalem
516BC	New Temple completed
486BC	Ahasuerus becomes king
483BC	Vashti deposed
479BC	Esther becomes queen
475BC	Haman becomes Prime Minister
474BC	Haman's decree
473BC	1st Feast of Purim

Lesson One:
Choices and Consequences

Esther 1

Choice One: Inward Honesty

Fill in the blanks as a review by referring to the chapter and verse given in the brackets [].

BACKGROUND INFORMATION:

TIME: 521 B.C. (_____ year of King Ahasuerus' reign) [1:3]

WHERE: Shushan, the _____ [1:2]

WHO: King _____ [1:2]

WHAT: Two feasts [1:3] (For all the _____, servants, nobles) [1:3]

1. What was King Ahasuerus doing? "_____ the riches of his glorious kingdom" [1:4]
2. What MAJOR attitude do you think directed the king's actions? _____
3. How long was the feast? _____ days (*one score = 20*) [1:4]

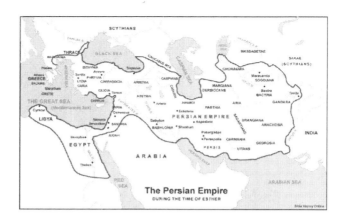

The Persian Empire
DURING THE TIME OF ESTHER

King Ahasuerus reigned from Ethiopia to India. He ruled a great kingdom. Is it still a powerful kingdom? No—it's all divided! It was one of the oldest kingdoms known to man and lasted longer than any other kingdom, but it's gone! The beautiful palace, the pavements of marble, the colorful hangings described in verses five to seven have vanished long ago.

APPLICATION:
CHOICES AND CONSEQUENCES

What are we laboring for? Do we put all of our time into making ourselves and our families more comfortable? Is that a bad thing? Not necessarily, but we do need to keep **our focus on the eternal.**

1 Peter 3:4

"But let it be the hidden man of the _____,
in that which is not _____,
even the ornament of a meek and quiet spirit,
which is in the sight of God of _____ price."

What is it in your life that may be crowding out those eternal things of greater importance? What gets in the way of your devotion to God, whether that devotion translates into church attendance, membership, baptism, devotions, scripture memory, prayer, or whatever God wants you to do? _____

VASHTI'S CHOICE:

1. What was Vashti, the queen doing at this time? [1:9]

   _____
   _____

2. Where was she? In the royal palace, which _____ to King Ahasuerus! [1:9] (Interesting that it is stated in this way! I wonder if she owned anything. Remember this for later when we see that the king offered to give Esther up to half the

kingdom! Does this tell us something about Vashti's character?)

What similarities we see between their society and ours! For example, notice verse eight:

> *"And the drinking was according to the law;*
> *none did compel:*
> *for so the king had appointed*
> *to all the officers of his house,*
> *that they should do*
> ***according to every man's pleasure."***

These were "civilized" revelers! Everyone was personally accountable for his drinking. Today, we don't usually hear anyone condemning drinking; we just want people to be aware of the dangers! The same is true of other vices in our society.

The women had their OWN party!   There's nothing new under the sun. The women's liberation movement has existed for thousands of years!

I share all this to say that Esther and other believers faced many of the same issues that we face today, and there is help for us in this little book.

1. King Ahasuerus sends seven eunuchs or servants to bring Vashti to his party. Why?

Because she was _____, "or fair to look on." [1:11]

2. Queen Vashti's response? _____ [1:12]
3. King Ahasuerus' response? _____ as a hornet!

(Have you ever met a mad hornet? I have! I was walking through the woods one day as a teen, and I must have been too close to its nest. For whatever the reason, unknown to me, that hornet came after me in no uncertain terms. There is no sting like that of a mad hornet!)

Should she have obeyed? Matthew Henry first takes a hard look at King Ahasuerus:

> *"It was against the custom of the Persians for the women to appear in public, and he put a great hardship upon her when he did not **court**, but **command** her to do so uncouth a thing, and make her a show. If he had not been put out of the possession of himself by drinking to excess, he would not have done such a thing, but would have been angry at any one that should have mentioned it. **When the wine is in, the wit is out, and men's reason departs from them.**"*

Should she have obeyed? Look at Matthew Henry's account of her choice:

> "Had she come, while it was evident that she did it in pure obedience, it would have been no reflection upon her modesty, nor a bad example. The thing was not in itself sinful, and therefore **to obey would have been more her honour than to be so precise.**"

Did God have a plan?   YES! In fact, Proverbs 16:4 says:

> "The LORD hath made _____ things for himself: yea, even the _____ for the day of evil."

Can God use one person's disobedience to help someone else? _____!

Vashti certainly had enough reasons not to obey the king's command, but **obedience is not determined by fairness!**

APPLICATION:
CHOICES AND CONSEQUENCES

Where do you have trouble obeying? We live in an age where we are sometimes encouraged NOT to obey, especially our husbands! Little did Vashti know how much her disobedience would cost her! Perhaps she did know and was glad to be gone! Whatever the situation, choices do have consequences, and we cannot determine what they are or how severe they will be. Does any addict know that he may lose his family when he takes a few extra pills? Does the parent ever consider that a bad habit will become a child's lifestyle? Can missing one or two...or three church services lead to a life of indifference towards God, or worse yet: a child with a hard heart towards God?

A favorite preacher of mine says,

"Sin will <u>always</u> take you
further than you wanted to go
and cost you more than you want to pay."

True Riches...we haven't gotten to the "meat" of this devotional yet, but where do your true riches lie? Take a look at your schedule, and you may find your answer!

I need to spend less time _____

I need to spend more time_____

To make this happen, I will _____

_____

Prayer is the greatest weapon you have for success. You may also need an accountability partner. Why is Weight Watchers so successful? **ACCOUNTABILITY!** I will ask _____ to be my accountability/prayer partner. (Optional, but a great idea! ☺)

Song of Solomon 2:15
"Take us the foxes, the little foxes,
that spoil the vines:
for our vines have tender grapes."

It was one little word that derailed Vashti's future: the little word NO! It's a word we should use **often** to our own flesh, and one that we should **NEVER** use towards God or our conscience!

Lesson Two:
Esther's Testimony

Esther 2:5 – 20
Choice Two: Submission

Part One: Man's Solution

Vashti's gone. After the party was over King Ahasuerus sought the council of his wise men and the highest princes about his situation. [1:13, 14] The wise men's decree was for Vashti to be removed [1:19]. What was the reason:

> *"For the deed of the queen*
> *should come abroad unto _____ women,*
> *so that they shall _____ their _____.*
> *Thus shall their arise much*
> *_____ and _____."* [1:17]

Wow! These are strong words: despise, wrath, contempt. Do you think they had a reason to worry? ____

Are you in a position of leadership like Vashti? _____ Perhaps you are not a queen ☺, but we should never forget that we ARE princesses–a child of the King! We are all leaders! We can all find someone who is following us and our example whether we like it or not.

List someone who looks up to you: _____
It may bother you to think that others are following you. You may say, "I didn't ask for that," but remember John 15:16a:

> "Ye have not chosen me,
> but I [God] have _____ you,
> and ordained you,
> that ye should go and bring forth fruit..."

As mothers and women in our churches and communities, we have responsibilities. God never chooses us to do anything without equipping us as well to be successful IN HIS EYES.

The leaders of Persia had an understanding of the queen's influence and example. Often, we ignore our responsibilities and just "let live." As Christian women, we have a special calling to be all that God wants us to be. Notice, I didn't say all that sister "so-and-so" is. God has a perfect design for **your** life. How exciting! Seeking the Lord's will for your life and doing it will bring such great joy!

When we walk with the Lord
in the light of His word,
what a glory He sheds on our way.
While we do His good will,
He abides with us still,
And with all who will TRUST AND OBEY.

TRUST AND OBEY, for there's no other way
To be happy in Jesus,
but to TRUST AND OBEY.
- John H. Sammis

Notice who gives the king advice about what to do next: _____ [2:2] We need to be careful about where we go for advice! The servants suggest an all-out beauty contest. All applicants must fulfill three requirements. [2:3]

        1. _____
        2. _____
        3. _____

The ultimate goal:

_____[2:4]

Winner takes all—she IS the queen!
"And the thing _____ the king;
and he did so." [2:4b]

Well, THAT is a good reason! It sounds like the modern day saying: "If it feels good, do it." It doesn't sound like the type of reasoning that we would use, and yet I find that if I take a closer look at some of my decisions—that's exactly my reasoning! Think about the following examples:

1. I eat too much.
2. I don't finish a job.
3. I watch TV instead of calling a friend in need.
4. I never get to sorting out my dresser drawers.
5. We eat fast foods.

(**Rabbit trail**: Some of the best advice I ever received was this: If it takes less than two minutes to do something, DO IT! That way, you won't use up precious brain power to remember to do it later!)

I'm not saying that it is never right to relax in front of the TV, or eat fast food, but life needs to have a balance, and we need to be honest about our excuses or reasoning. If my actions are ruining my family's health, keeping me from ministering, or ruining my testimony for God all because "I did or didn't feel like it," then it is time to reevaluate my schedule and motives!

APPLICATION:

SUBMISSION 101

Several synonyms for this lovely word are: obedience, compliance, capitulation, surrender, acquiescence, deference, assent, **giving in.** An antonym is **resistance**!

We may not know Vashti's reasons for not being submissive; however, we might find some answers to our own faltering in this area by looking at another dear woman in the Bible: Eve.

God shows us three main reasons why we choose to follow our way instead of following, or submitting, to the authorities in our lives.

"And when the woman saw
that the tree was good for _____,
and that it was pleasant to the _____,
and a tree to be desired to make one _____,
she took of the fruit thereof, and did eat,
and gave also unto her husband with her;
and he did eat." Genesis 3:6

Here it is, the big three:

1. **The lust of the flesh**: Eve wanted to enjoy the forbidden fruit.

2. **The lust of the eyes**: She saw that is was beautiful and desirable to look upon.
3. **The pride of life:** She believed Satan and desired worldly wisdom.

Like each of us, Vashti was responsible for her own actions; however, her friends certainly fueled her fire of defiance.

Be careful who you run with. I can see Vashti surrounded by her friends. I'm sure she got no encouragement to obey the king! They probably had plenty of reasons for her to disobey the command. Here again, there's nothing new under the sun.

A scene from *Fireproof* (http://www.fireproofthemovie.com) shows Katherine surrounded by her friends who are giving her much the same advice that Vashti probably got. However, in both cases, those friends were not the ones destroying their marriages or losing their homes, if they hadn't been destroyed already!

Esther was a young woman that God was about to use greatly. We have already seen one prong of His planned deliverance: removing Vashti from her position of influence. Now, let us look of God's man for the hour!

Part Two: A certain Jew named Mordecai

What do we know about the man, Mordecai?

1. He was a descendant of _____. Notice that Mordecai's lineage is given [2:5]. That's quite amazing considering the time in which he lived. How many Jews had lost their tribal identity? Notice he is a son of Kish [2:5], which makes him a relative of Saul, the first king of Israel! As a descendant of Kish, Mordecai would carry with him a sense of royalty.

2. He is Esther's _____. [2:7] He "brought up Hadassah" for she was an orphan. At first glance, her Hebrew name doesn't seem to bear any great significance: it means myrtle tree, or one among the myrtle trees. However, at a closer look, the name was given to the righteous, because the tree was good and gave off a pleasant smell. (Here we have another hidden challenge: Do we sweeten the atmosphere when we come into a room or sour

it?!) Her submission to this man moved her from among the myrtle trees to the heavens: Esther, her Babylonian name, means star!

3. He is a _____ [2:6] I would think that this fact would be understood, but it is significant. Mordecai and Hadassah were carried away into a foreign land of Babylon by Nebuchadnezzar over a hundred years before our story takes place. Many of the Jews just melded into the Babylonian culture and forgot their heritage. Not true about our heroes!

4. "He _____ _____ Hadassah" [2:7] When her parents were dead, he took her in, not only as a guardian, but he treated her as his own _____.

We don't know how Hadassah was selected for the king's search for a queen. We are told that she was *"fair and beautiful."* Verse eight just says that *"she was brought also unto the king's house."*

Throughout this story, one amazing attribute rises to the top in Esther: her submission. She submits to EVERYBODY (except for the bad guy!).

APPLICATION:

SUBMISSION 102

1. **Submission to Mordecai**

   Daughters, do you realize that you are practicing for marriage in the way in which you submit to your father? Remember, submission is only difficult when we do NOT agree!

   - He *"charged her that she should not"* reveal her Jewish heritage.
   - Are you ever asked to keep a secret? Is it submitting to keep that secret? Yes or no? _____

2. **Submission to Hegai, keeper of the women**

   Our parallel today would be an employer or coworker. How are our submission skills showing out there in the world? Again, may I say that submission is only difficult when we don't agree! Do you have an unfair boss?

   Here it is, ladies: *"Esther obtained favour in the sight of _____ them that looked upon her."* [2:15] Now that's a tall order! Let's review some of our synonyms for submission:

   obedience   compliance   capitulation

surrender   deference   assent

giving in   acquiescence

- Would these words describe your character?_____
- Is it possible that these attributes would make us more favorable in the eyes of others? _____
- Would our relationships be improved if we tried to implement some of these into our daily walk? _____
- Take a moment and plug in some of the above words into the following sentences:
  - ➤ I need to practice _____with _____ (person)
  - ➤ I need to work on my _____ in _____ (circumstances).

3. **Submission to Ahasuerus**

So far, the information we have on this king is:

- He gives long extravagant parties
- He takes advice from his underlings

28

- He makes decisions based on pleasure
- He favors Esther

Later, we will read that he likes Esther so much, that he's willing to give her half the kingdom; however, we will also see that submission to him does not mean just submitting to a husband—she is also submitting to a king!

There's a special lesson to those of us who are in a ministry position. Our submission to our husbands, or the lack thereof, can make or break his ministry, which is ultimately God's ministry. Remember, submission is only difficult when we disagree! Be careful how you treat your husbands, dear pastor's wife, when you are with others! *"For unto whomsoever much is given, of him shall be much required"* (Luke 12:48) Oh, how they watch us! It is our responsibility to give them a good example to follow! Keep an eye on Esther's example—she is the expert!

Lesson Three:
The Conspiracy and the Bad Guy

Esther 2:21 – 3:15
Choice Three: Trust

How many times do events happen in our lives and we credit it to coincidence? Does anything truly ever happen by coincidence for the believer? How strongly do we believe that God is in control of our lives? Think of Jesus' statement that even the hairs on our heads are numbered by God (Matthew 10:30), and that He sees when the sparrow falls (Matthew 10:29). Do we serve an **omnipotent, omniscient** God? Can He do **anything**? Does He know **everything**?

The Plot Thickens!

Read chapter 2:21-23. Remember the first time you read Esther's story? We might have ask, "Why is this in here?" This passage would seem like random information if we didn't know the rest of the story. Oh, may we never read anything in God's Word and think it is random! God has a purpose for every *"jot and tittle."*(Matthew 5:18)

Does it do anything for you to know that the mighty Creator God, Ruler of the Universe has plans for **your** day? At this very moment He may be allowing circumstances (that you are totally unaware of) to be occurring, which will play an important part of your life!

When we moved to Pennsylvania from Virginia, we had no idea what God was doing. In fact, in January of that year, the former pastor had resigned after thirty-five years of faithful service. At the same time, we were just beginning to sense that God was moving us on. What a joy to walk in the presence of an all-knowing King! When the darkest times came that summer, I would often sing these words:

What tho the way be lonely,
and dark shadows fall,
I know where're He leads me,
My Father plans it all.
*There may be sunshine **tomorrow**,*
Shadows break and flee,
Twill be the way He chooses:
My Father's plan for me.

~ H. H. Pierson

I knew that God was planning our days for us, and that at any time the tide could change—and it did! That may not be much comfort to you if you are in an impossible situation. Perhaps you have just lost a loved one. That situation cannot change! But as we will see later on, even in the face of death, God is there orchestrating our paths! And what is our verse for all of this: 2 Corinthians 5:7 Look it up and take a minute to write it down:

_____

_____

_____

_____

Problem # 1: Long Lost Enemies

Chapter three starts with the king promoting a man named Haman "*above _____ the princes that were with him.*" [3:1] Notice Haman's heritage: "*Haman the son of Hammedatha the Agagite*" [1:1] If you have a study Bible, you may notice a cross reference to 1 Sam. 15: 8: "*and he [King Saul] took Agag the king of the Amalekites alive, and utterly destroyed all the people with the edge of the sword.*"

Evidently, Haman was a descendent of Agag whom Saul was supposed to slay. Interesting, we now have two descendants once again meeting in conflict. Do you think that Haman knew that Mordecai was a descendant of Saul? Just that Mordecai was a Jew was probably enough for Haman. Can you see why Haman had such a hatred for the Jews even before Esther and Mordecai entered the scene!

Problem #2: To Bow or Not to Bow

We see in verse two that all the king's servants who sat at the king's gate were to bow to Haman. *"But Mordecai bowed _____, nor did him _____."* [3:2] Even though all the servants tried to persuade Mordecai to "follow the rules," he continued to refuse. Look how often they spoke to him about the matter: _____ [3:4]

APPLICATION:
TRUST 101

How often do others try to persuade you to "bow to this world?" What exactly does that mean? Any time we feel pressure to do what everyone else is doing even though it goes against our own convictions, we stand in the place where Mordecai stood! Remember, this was the KING'S command! It wasn't just peer pressure. These servants knew that there would be consequences for Mordecai's actions! They obviously cared for him and didn't want him to get into trouble.

Can you think of a verse in the New Testament that addresses this issue? Take a look at Acts 4:19:

"But Peter and John answered and said unto them, whether it be _____ in the sight of _____ to hearken unto you _____ than unto God, judge ye."

Obviously as a Jew, Mordecai couldn't or wouldn't bow to anyone but God. Consider the following:

God's Law	Man's Opinions
Ephesians 6:1 *"Children obey your parents..."*	"...only when they are right"
Ephesians 5:22 *"Wives, submit...to your own husbands, as unto the Lord."*	"...when I agree with him!" (It's only hard to submit when I don't agree!) Did I say that before? ☺
Luke 6:27 *"...Love your enemies"*	"...when it benefits me."
1Peter 1:15 *"... be ye holy in all manner of conversation."*	"...just as long as I don't stick out!"

Where to you bow? When is it hard for you to obey God?   Does your life style reflect a submissive spirit to God's Law? What do I mean? Here are some examples. On which side do your decisions fall?

Problem #3: A Two-sided Affair

The decision has been made: kill all the Jews! What an enormous price to pay for one Jewish man's decision not to bow! It shows the height of Haman's arrogance!   But Haman was not aware of God's promises! Long before Haman was born, God had directly promised Abraham blessings on those that blessed him and cursing on those that cursed him:

> *"And I will bless them that bless thee,*
> *and curse him that curseth thee:*
> *and in thee shall all families*
> *of the earth be blessed."* Genesis 12: 3

So even though it seemed like a disaster for the Jews, it is also a disaster waiting to happen for Haman! Satan is certainly using Haman in his plan, but both are only pawns in the hand of the Master Strategist!

In verse seven, we see that the lot is cast to decide what month and day the Jews would be destroyed. Interesting that the lot is cast during the first month, and the month chosen is the twelfth, giving God plenty of time to work out the details! (Not that He needed it!)

Should we cast lots to make decisions? It certainly is one way to make choices. Even the apostles used the lot to choose the twelfth apostle after Judas' death. It would require a lot of prayer and even more faith to trust God in making the decision!

Notice the following verse:

"The lot is cast into the lap;
but the _____ disposing thereof
*is of the _____."*Proverb 16:33

What a blessing to know that even in the hands of the wicked, such as Haman, God is the One who chose the time!

Problem #4: The Death Sentence

Notice Haman's statement to the king concerning the Jews:

"And Haman said unto king Ahasuerus,
There is a certain _____ scattered abroad
and dispersed among the people
in all the provinces of thy kingdom;
and their laws are _____ from all people;
neither _____ they the king's laws:
therefore
it is not for the king's _____ to suffer them."
Esther 3: 8

Which of the following statements of Haman are true?

1. *True False* There were a certain people scattered throughout the king's kingdom.
2. *True False* Their laws were different from the people of Persia.
3. *True False* They did not keep Persia's laws.
4. *True False* The kingdom would be better off without them.

Haman is twisting the truth to make his plea more concrete. Do we ever do that? Do we build our case with a few extra embellishments to bend the verdict our way? Please excuse the example, but an image of two Siamese cats just came to mind! In the movie *Lady and the Tramp*, Lady, the Cocker Spaniel, is falsely accused of making a mess of the aunt's living room as well as attacking her favored pets; when in fact, the cats destroyed the room then lie on their backs howling as if they had just been attacked!

Let's be careful to be honest first in our own hearts, then honest with others!

"Wherefore putting away lying,
Speak every man _____
with his _____:
for we are members one of another."
(Remember, neighbors can live under the same roof as we do!) Ephesians 4:25

The King's Command

"And the king said unto Haman,
The silver is given to thee,
the people also, to do with them
as it seemeth _____ to thee."
"The posts went out, being hastened
by the king's commandment,

and the decree was given in Shushan the palace.
And the king and Haman sat down to _____;
but the city Shushan was _____."

Esther 3: 11, 15

Here was a great test for not only the Jews, but the people of Shushan. Why this sudden act of destruction? No doubt many innocent people would be killed, Jews and Persians, as those who were sent to destroy were also promised the spoils! It was certainly time to trust the LORD!

APPLICATION:
TRUST 102

Have you ever been blind-sided by the unexpected? How did you react? Denial? Frustration? Anger? Fear? How should we react? Here again are a few words from one of our Bible heroes:

"And [Job] said,
Naked came I out of my mother's womb,
and naked shall I return thither:
the LORD _____, and the LORD hath
_____ away;
_____ be the name of the LORD." Job 1:21

There are many passages where God's people praise His name for His deliverance or protection, but in this account, Job has just lost everything. There is no sign of deliverance. There is no hope of change. All is lost! **Oh, to be able to trust God like that!**

Meditate on these quotes. What a blessing they will be! Then look up the following verses and fill in the blanks. If you are struggling with trust, memorize some of the verses. The Lord will bring them to mind when you need them most! Aren't you glad we have the **Living Word** to guide us, and the Holy Spirit to be our aid?

"You may trust the Lord too little,
but you can never trust Him too much".
Anonymous

"Beware of despairing about yourself;
you are commanded to put your trust in God,
and not in yourself." St. Augustine

"We trust as we love, and where we love.
If we love Christ much, surely we shall trust Him
much." Brooks

"All I have seen teaches me to trust the Creator
for all I have not seen." Emerson

"Don't try to hold God's hand; let Him hold yours.
Let Him do the holding, and you the trusting."
Webb-Peploe

Pro. 14: 26   *"In the _____ of the LORD is*
_____ confidence: and his
children shall have a place of
_____."

Isaiah 26: 4   *"_____ ye in the LORD for*
_____: for in the LORD JEHOVAH
is everlasting _____:

Nahum 1:7   *"The LORD is _____,*
a _____ hold in the day of
_____; and he
_____ them that
trust in him."

Psalm 36: 7   *"How excellent is thy_____,*
O God! therefore the children of men
put their trust under the shadow of
thy _____."

I Peter 5:7   *"Casting _____ your care upon him;*
for he careth for _____."

41

Psalm 9: 10   *"And they that _____ thy name will put their trust in thee: for thou, LORD, hast not forsaken them that _____ thee."*

II Cor. 1:10   *"Who _____ us from so great a death, and doth _____: in whom we trust that he will yet _____ us;"*

Proverbs 3: 5   *"Trust in the LORD with _____ thine heart; and lean not unto thine _____ understanding."*

Lesson Four:
The Golden Scepter – Stage for Success

Esther 4
Choice: My Mission

Actions

It's been five years now that Esther has been living in the palace as queen. I'm sure it took a while to learn all about all of her responsibilities. She is queen, and her king loves her...and they lived happily ever after! Well, this truly is a story with all the right ingredients: impossible situations, a beautiful heroine and of course, the bad guy!

I would think that Esther knew Haman. I'm sure he was especially nice to the queen, just in case he might need a favor sometime in the future! As we have already seen, Haman thinks of only one thing: Haman! Little might Esther have realized the impact he would have on her and her people!

How serious was the situation?

"And in _____ province, whithersoever the king's commandment and his decree came, there

43

was _____ mourning among the Jews, and
_____, and _____, and _____;
and _____ lay in sackcloth and ashes." Esther 4:3

Can you imagine if the decree was sent forth to kill all Christians? Some countries have faced that scenario in our lifetime. If by some underhanded dealings like this, we were all sentenced to die, what would you or I do? I wonder how many would give up their faith or go into hiding?

"...Nevertheless when the Son of man cometh,
shall he find _____ on the earth?" Luke 18: 8

Matthew Henry says,

> *"Now, when he comes, will he find faith on the earth? The question implies a strong negation: No, he will not; he himself foresees it."*

How sad. This verse always challenges me to stand faithful, no matter how hard it gets! May it do the same for you! Remember, "hard" may be different for you than it is for others. "Hard" for you might be facing a full schedule on Sunday or Wednesday which ultimately crowds out church. Or, for someone else, it may be the struggle to be consistent with devotions, being a witness, prayer. Whatever the challenges in your Christian walk, remember where we started this devotional:

WHAT NEEDS TO CHANGE
FOR ME TO BECOME MORE LIKE CHRIST?

Reactions

Esther hears what is happening, but doesn't know what is going on.

"So Esther's maids and her chamberlains came
and told it her.
Then was the queen exceedingly grieved;
and she sent _____
to clothe Mordecai, and to take away his
_____ from him: but he received it _____."
Esther 4:4

She tries to help Mordecai and encourage him. She's probably already heard about his refusal to bow and is trying to "save his skin!" Little does she yet realize the seriousness of the situation!

Are we guilty of the same thing? How often do we go about our business forgetting that millions have been condemned to eternal death unless they heard and embrace the truth about Jesus Christ! The sad part about our situation is that many are totally unaware of the pending danger themselves or choose to ignore it. Sadder still are those who choose to cling to false hopes that have been given to them by false teachers!

APPLICTAION:
MY MISSION 101

What is our reaction? Do we follow Esther's example here and try to cover up the truth? Or do we tell them? Dear Sister in Christ, I hope you are busy getting the Word out! Let's list some ways that you can get out the Gospel or soften the ground for others to receive God's Word when It is given:

Example: bake something for a lost neighbor

1. _____
2. _____
3. _____
4. _____
5. _____
6. _____

"Then called Esther for _____,
one of the king's chamberlains,
whom he had appointed to attend upon her,
and gave him a commandment to Mordecai, to
know what it was, and why it was." Esther 4:5

Isn't it nice to have friends you can turn to? Do you remember this name? Hatach befriended Esther right from the start! Be thankful for good friends! Hatach was probably not a believer, we don't know; but he was a good friend. Do your friends know that you are a believer, especially your unsaved friends? If not, pray for opportunities to share your testimony with them. Telling them about the circumstances in which God drew you to Him, is one of the best ways to open that door of witness!

Hatach goes out into the streets and finds Mordecai, who tells him everything that has happened. He also tells him a little piece of information that helps to make sense of the King's decree.

"And Mordecai told him of all that had happened
unto him, and of the sum of the _____
that Haman had promised to pay to the king's
_____ for the Jews, to destroy them."
Esther 4: 7

The Persians had just lost a major war which cost the king's kingdom a great deal. Haman was well aware of this when he approached the king and offered to pay a hefty sum of **his own money** to destroy the Jews! Such hatred of God's people! It staggers the imagination! But can we turn around these thoughts and learn something?

How much am I willing to "pay" to destroy Satan's kingdom? Will I make a meal, visit an unlovely person, greet a visitor, join the choir, or clean the church? All of these things and any other task that furthers God's kingdom are also destroying Satan's! What a lovely thought! ☺

"Pappy" Mordecai also sees things a little more clearly than the queen!

" *Also he gave him the copy of the writing of the decree that was given at Shushan to destroy them, to shew it unto Esther, and to declare it unto her, and to _____ her that she _____ go in unto the king, to make _____ unto him, and to make _____ before him for ____ people.*"[4:8]

I wonder if this statement got the grape vine humming:

"Are you sure that's what he said?"

"Yes! I'm sure. He said HER people."

"But what did he mean?"

"Her means HER! The queen is a JEW!"

"But that's impossible! Surely our king wouldn't have married a Jew! We'd better have a recount!" (Sorry—got a little political there!)

Have you ever thought about how old Esther is through all of this? One study said that she was about ten or eleven when King Ahasuerus took the throne. She would then be thirteen or fourteen when taken! At the time of this incident, she would be around eighteen or nineteen years of age!

Sometimes I wonder if our society would do our young people a service by letting them take responsibility for their actions sooner. The average young person doesn't start to pay his own way until age twenty-two if he has attended college. Even then, some parents continue to hover over them and keep them at home.

Esther is making the greatest decision of her life, probably before she is twenty years old! Her response to Mordecai:

"_____ the king's servants, and the _____
of the king's provinces, do know, that _____,
whether man or woman,
shall come unto the king into the inner court,
who is not called,
there is one law of his to put him to death,
except such to whom the king
shall hold out the golden sceptre,
that he may live:
but I have not been called to come in
unto the king these thirty days." [4:11]

She has all her reasons in order! All the people understood her dilemma; certainly her own dear Mordecai would understand! There was nothing that she could do! She would possibly die if the king was in one of those moods! After all, the whole incident with the last queen wasn't that far back in history or in the minds of everyone!

Here we have the most famous discourse in the Book of Esther:

1. Mordecai warns her that she will not escape this judgment:
"Then Mordecai commanded to answer Esther,
Think not with thyself that thou shalt _____ in
the king's house, more than _____ the Jews." [4:13]

2. God keeps His promises:

"For if thou altogether holdest thy peace
at this time,
then shall there enlargement and deliverance arise
to the Jews from _____ place;
but thou and thy father's house shall be destroyed...
[4:14a]

3. God has a plan:

"...and who knoweth whether thou art
_____ to the kingdom
for such a _____ as this?" [4:14b]

When the going gets tough...

    ...the tough get going.

    ...we go home to Mom.

    ...we throw up our hands in despair.

    ...we blame someone.

    ...we fast.

Look at Esther's response:

"Go, gather together all the Jews that are
present in Shushan, and fast ye for me, and neither
eat nor drink three days, night or day: I also and my
maidens will fast likewise; and so will I go in unto the
king, which is not according to the law: and if I
perish, I perish." [4:16]

WOW! I don't know about you, but the most I have ever fasted was twenty-four hours! Three days! Not even any water! She was in a desperate situation. You know the old saying:

"Desperate times call for desperate measures."

Here is some interesting information about fasting:

"Although the text doesn't specifically mention that Esther's fast was for the purpose of prayer, Scripture clearly links the two together. In Oriental culture fasting was one of many ways a person expressed mourning. Although Scripture does not command fasting, it does mention it in a way that strongly stresses its importance. In the Sermon on the Mount, Jesus does not say, 'If you fast...' but 'When you fast....' Scriptural fasts can last for part or all of a day, several days, or even as long as forty days, and can mean doing without all food and water, food only, or abstaining from certain foods for a time (as in the Nazarite vow). *Fasting does not twist the arm of God to get Him to do what we would like.* It simply helps us to make seeking Him our highest priority. **When our seeking of God is more important to us than even our daily** needs, we are in a position of sensitivity to Him so that we can hear what he wants to say to us.

The pains of hunger in a fast are regular reminders to return to prayer and seek the face of God. As we will see very soon, a lot of consequential things occurred during this three-day delay. We must be ever watchful of running ahead of God and the work He desires to do on our behalf." Barber, Rasnake, Shepherd, *Following God: Women of the Bible* p.112, 113

"So Mordecai went his way, and did according to all that Esther had commanded him." [4:17]

The wheels were turning. Action was taking place. All the Jews were fasting including Esther and her chambermaids. And God was doing His part as well! Esther had a mission!

APPLICATION:
MY MISION 102

What is your mission, and have you successfully prepared for it? What would be important enough to you for you to fast for three days? This lesson is a great rebuke to me! Take a moment and list some things that would warrant your fasting:

_____

_____

_____

_____

It is easy to stay so busy with all the tasks necessary to keep a household going, that we lose sight of our "mission." Again, what is your mission? Is it to nurture the little people in your life: children or grandchildren? Is it to be the best example you can be to an unsaved spouse or other loved ones? Maybe your mission is to have victory over sin in a certain area of your life. What would you like to see God accomplish in your life?

Esther was in partnership with all those people who were fasting *as well as with God*!

"For we are labourers together _____ God:
_____ are God's husbandry,
_____ are God's building." 1Corinthians 3:9

What a partnership! Have you ever played a game and you were stuck with a poor partner? Maybe he didn't know how to play well or he just didn't care. Here we see that we, as well as Esther, are God's partner. I think we got the better end of the bargain!!

We are his husbandry—that literally means farm. He's busy digging and planting and pruning and harvesting our lives! Paul then uses the word "building." We are God's architecture! He is designing us! He's pounding and hammering and sawing and nailing and painting and tearing down and...I think you get the picture! We are HIS mission!

"A man's heart deviseth his way:
but the LORD directeth his steps." Proverbs 16: 9

Lesson Five:
True Riches – True Motives

Esther 5
Choice Five: My Focus

Obedient Servant

"If I perish, I perish." Those were Esther's words, and now she has been fasting with the entire Jewish population in Shushan for three days; and she has prepared her heart, which is the most important part. Now let's look at how she prepares herself outwardly:

What did Esther put on [5:1] her _____

_____

Appearance does matter! Do you remember a few years ago, when the Northwestern University lacrosse team were rebuked for appearing before the president in flip flops? Apparel is an issue that continues to come under hot debate in Christian circles. What do we do with it?

1.   Ignore it
2.   Split the church over it
3.   Let it wrinkle our spirits
4.   Go to God's Word:

*"One man esteemeth
one day above another:
another esteemeth every day alike.
Let every man be **fully persuaded
in his own mind**."* Romans 14:5

It might be good for you to take a moment and think about why you do dress the way you do. What is influencing you: peer pressure, the world, your comfort, your convictions, other's convictions, your weight...

Let me share my testimony:

I was saved when I was seventeen years old, but I wasn't "sanctified" in any sense of the word until much later. In other words, I was not hearing strong Bible teaching or being challenged about my Christian walk. So, going to class at college in shorts and a halter top was the smartest thing to do if it was hot!

After we were married and started attending a Bible preaching church, I started noticing how others dressed at church—especially those that I looked up to. As a child, I can remember the big shake up in our denominational church when some of the ladies started to wear pant suits to church.

(I'm dating myself!) Perhaps that is why I felt I needed to be in a dress at church at that point.

Later, I taught kindergarten at the Christian school affiliated with our church. I remember being at the State Farm Show (we lived near Harrisburg, Pennsylvania at the time) and was wearing slacks. I was worried that one of my little kindergarten girls might see the way that I was dressed, and it might confuse her. I didn't want to be living a "double" standard.

So, from then on, unless I'm playing in the snow ☺ or am involved in some other activity that requires pants for modesty or warmth, I'm usually in a dress or skirt. Another factor is that I know my husband prefers me in a dress. It also helps me to be more lady-like, and I need all the help I can get in that area!

So what is influencing me in my decision?
1.   The testimony of others that I respected
2.   Childhood memories
3.   My testimony towards others
4.   My own convictions (no double standard)
5.   My husband's preferences
6.   My own preference
7.   Honoring my Lord and Savior

I'll often tease with teen girls who are shocked that I would roller skate in a skirt, that if the pioneer women crossed this country in a skirt, I think that I can roller skate in one! ☺

Do I go to the Bible on this decision and quote Deuteronomy 22: 5:

> *"The woman shall not wear that*
> *which pertaineth unto a man,*
> *neither shall a man put on a woman's garment:*
> *for all that do so are abomination*
> *unto the LORD thy God."*

No. Why? Because when this verse was written, men and women wore tunics that looked very similar. The verse is a warning not to confuse the sexes; in other words, men are to be men and women to be women. We all need that admonition in the day in which we live! My point:

> *"One man esteemeth*
> *one day above another:*
> *another esteemeth every day alike.*
> *Let every man be **fully persuaded***
> ***in his own mind**."*
> *Romans 14:5*

You must be fully persuaded what the Lord would have for you. Do others influence you? Certainly, we do not live in a vacuum. Do we need to wrestle with this? I believe so. Here is another verse on this issue:

1 Samuel 16: 7
"But the LORD said unto Samuel,
Look not on his countenance,
or on the height of his stature;
because I have refused him:
for the LORD seeth not as man seeth;
for man looketh
on the outward appearance,
but the LORD looketh on the heart."

We often quote this verse as an excuse to be unconcerned about our appearance, but look at the bold print part. **People may not see our hearts because of how we are dressed. We need to be concerned with both, just like Esther.** She had her heart prepared, but then she went to great lengths to prepare her outward appearance, and it made a difference!

Seeing women in dresses is a dying art. I can't imagine either of my grandmothers in pants. Take a look at any book published before 1950 or any movie portraying that era—all the women are in dresses! We can speak loudly by the way we are dressed.

Am I saying that you are less than holy if you wear slacks? Absolutely not! I share all of this not to push any of you into "my standards," but to challenge you to be what God wants you to be! Only YOU can answer what that means in your life.

Clueless Fool

Esther has made her petition to the king: a banquet for the king and Haman. They make haste to come and then are asked to come again tomorrow for another banquet. (These people really love to eat!) Haman leaves with a bounce in his step...until...

"Then went Haman forth that day _____
and with a _____ heart:
but when Haman saw Mordecai in the king's gate,
that he stood not up,
nor moved for him,
he was full of _____ against Mordecai."
[5:9]

Here sits faithful Mordecai–faithful to the end, even though that end looks rather bleak! I wonder if Mordecai could see the gallows being built and hear the hammers ringing from his spot by the gate.

Meanwhile, Haman calls for a brag party. He sends for his wife and his friends to come over and tells them about his wonderful life!

"And Haman told them
of the glory of his_____,
and the multitude of his _____,
and all the things
wherein the king had _____ him,
and how he had advanced him
_____ the princes and servants of the king.
Haman said moreover,
Yea, Esther the queen did let _____ man
come in with the king
unto the banquet that she had prepared
but _____;
and tomorrow am I invited
unto her also with the king." [5:11, 12]

List Haman's accomplishments:

1. Glory of his _____
2. Multitude of his _____
3. The king's _____
4. His advancement above all _____ and _____
5. _____ initiation to him and the king

"Yet all this availeth me _____,
so long as I see Mordecai the Jew
sitting at the king's gate." [5:13]

GUILTY!!! Oh, how many times am I just as guilty as Haman! God pours out His blessings upon my life and all I see is what is missing! Why is it, that if a full size sheet is hanging on the line with one tiny spot on it, our eye sees only the spot?

Let's take a moment to list the trials and blessings in our lives. For every trial listed, list two blessings!

TRIALS	BLESSINGS	BLESSINGS

Count your blessings! Remember them in your hour of need. What a strength they will be to you!

"And I said, This is my _____:
but I will remember the _____ of the right hand
of the most High.
I will remember the works of the LORD:
surely I will _____ thy wonders of old."
(in my life !)
Psalm 77:10,11
63

This verse has been a stronghold for me over the years. Even this week, as I worried about a need in my life, God not only reminded me of past "rescues" that He has performed, but He sent the answer to my need within twenty-four hours!

> *"Oh that men would _____ the LORD*
> *for his _____,*
> *and for his _____ works*
> *to the children of men!"* Psalm 107:8

Look at Esther 5:14. Who suggests the gallows for Mordecai? _____, Haman's _____!!!

Can your husband or family rely on you to give good godly advice? _____

Do you go to God's Word when you are in doubt? If you are still not sure of an answer, do you go to the one who will give you a good, godly answer or to the one that will tell you what you want to hear?

I want to praise the Lord for my mom. I never went to her and complained about my husband, because she would always side with him! I never heard, "Poor Wanda! Yes, that Tom is a bully isn't he!"

I've tried to keep that attitude with my children as they are now married! It's not easy! We love our children and want to coddle them, but that isn't what they need! They need to hear the truth! Little did Haman's wife know that her own husband would be hanged on the gallows she suggested!

God's Providence

This is my favorite part of the story!

> *"On _____ night could not the king sleep,*
> *and he commanded to bring*
> *the book of records of the _____;*
> *and they were read before the king."* [6:1]

Why THAT night? **God!**
Why THAT book? **God!**

Little was the king aware of the reason that he could not sleep! He was unaware that the book chosen to make him sleepy would contain an incident that would change history!

> *"My God is so big! My God is so mighty!*
> *There's nothing my God cannot do!"*

65

Do you believe that? I love to pray for the impossible! As I pray, I remind the Lord that He is the God of the Impossible! (As if He didn't already know!! ☺)

"I say unto you,
Though he will not rise and give him,
because he is his friend,
yet because of his _____
he will rise and give him as many as he needeth.
And I say unto you,
Ask, and it shall be given you;
seek, and ye shall find; knock,
and it shall be opened unto you."
Luke 11: 8, 9

Importunity - *to **urge** or **beg** with **troublesome** persistence* ☺ Is that how you pray?

Why had Mordecai done this deed? (Read Esther 2:21-23 if you don't remember) It could have backfired on him and cost him his life! These were dangerous men! They tried to kill the king; they might have planned to get even with Mordecai as well!

Integrity - adherence to a code of values

Like Mordecai, our "code of values" is the Bible! We do what is right because it is the right thing to do!

A Bitter Pill

Well, actually, this may be my favorite part of the story! Haman is in the court quite early. He has come to speak to the king about hanging Mordecai! He has already presumptuously started to build the gallows! The king is just an afterthought to him! How self-absorbed he is; but God is still watching!

King Ahasuerus poses the question:

> *"What shall be done unto the man whom the king _____ to _____ ?*
> *Now Haman thought in his heart,*
> *To whom would the king delight to do honour more than to _____ ?"* [6:6]

WOW! Do we see arrogance? Then came the blow!

Read Esther 6:7-12. Can you picture this? Everyone knows by now about the hatred Haman has for Mordecai! Would there be anything more humiliating for Haman? God knows exactly what we need! We've just talked about the trials that we face. When those trials are of our own making because of sin in our lives, let God have His way!

APPLICATION:
MY FOCUS

Even though He may give us a bitter pill to swallow, remember Who is administering the medicine: the One who knows us better than we know ourselves; the One who has only our good in mind; the One who turns ashes into beauty!

"...to give unto them beauty for _____,
the oil of joy for _____,the garment of praise
for the spirit of _____;
that they might be called trees of _____,
the planting of the LORD, that he might be _____.
Isaiah 61:3

The last part of this verse is the greater part! We allow Him to give us ashes, and mourning, and heaviness that we might, by His grace, ALLOW Him to turn them into beauty, joy, and praise. Why? For His Glory!

Lesson Six:

Character of a King – A Watching World

Esther 7-9
Choice Six – My Witness

Yesterday brought a banquet of wine for the King and Haman, and then yet another invitation. We have seen Esther's side of this story: She and all of Jewry have been praying and fasting for the past three days. We have also seen Haman's side: He foolishly instructed the king concerning honor for whom the king delighted. He has boasted to his family only to be humiliated throughout Shushan by giving honor to Mordecai, his enemy, and then returning home again to receive a prophecy of doom from his wife and friends.

It reminds me of Amos 5:12:

> *"As if a man did flee from a lion,*
> *and a bear met him;*
> *or went into the house,*
> *and leaned his hand on the wall,*
> *and a serpent bit him."*

Talk about a bad day!!

As far as we can tell, King Ahasuerus was unaware of Esther or Haman's troubles. He was busy running the kingdom! Do you ever look around a room full of people and wonder what they have faced that day? Sometimes behind the smiles are a lot of difficulties.

How often are we so busy getting the job done that we don't notice the quivering chin or the sad eyes! Jude 22 says: *"And of some having _____, making a _____."* If there is one lesson we all could learn, it is this: **People** are more important than **things**. I often praise God for His awesome creation—I love the beauty of this world. But I was recently reminded that God's crowning creation is people! Take time to make a difference! No wonder James describes pure religion this way:

> *"Pure religion and undefiled before God*
> *and the Father is this,*
> *To _____ the fatherless and widows*
> *in their affliction,*
> *and to _____ himself unspotted*
> *from the world."*
> James 1:27

The Truth

Again, King Ahasuerus asks Esther to make her request, and offers her anything up to the half of the kingdom. Finally, the truth is revealed:

> *"Then Esther the queen answered and said,*
> *If I have found favour in thy sight. O king,*
> *and if it please the king,*
> let **my** _____ be given me at my petition, **and**
> **my** _____ at my request:
> *For we are sold, I and my people,*
> *to be destroyed, to be slain, and to perish.*
> *But if we had been sold*
> *for bondmen and bondwomen,*
> *I had held my tongue, although the enemy could not*
> *countervail the king's damage."* [7:3,4]

The king is totally caught off guard. He probably expected her to ask for riches or the advancement of a friend, but instead, she asks for her life! Who would be so presumptuous to execute the queen? Without hesitation, Esther points to Haman: the king's right-hand man!

Notice what she says: *"The adversary and enemy is this* _____ *Haman."*

Haman now sees Esther in a different light! Up until now, he has only thought of her as a quiet little

71

queen! He certainly responded correctly: *"Then Haman was _____ before the king and the queen."* [7:6]

We also see a different king than the one that we met in the beginning of this book! He has learned some lessons along the way. Could it be that he has even learned integrity just from watching his wife? Can others say the same about us? Can they see and learn something about our Savior just by watching our actions and reactions?

"And then the king arising from the banquet of wine in his wrath went into the palace _____..." [7:7] Why? Perhaps, to cool down and to think? How had he been such a fool not to see Haman's true character? He had been pulled right into Haman's evil plan, not thinking about the destruction of a guiltless nation which included his wife! Did the King even know that Esther was a Jew? We don't know, but he knows now that her life is in danger, and he has had a hand in it!

Unfortunately for Haman, he chooses this time to plead with Esther, falling *"upon the bed where on Esther was."* [7:8] The king enters the room and thinks the worst. Is Haman now going to force himself upon the queen? His wrath against Haman colors everything that Haman does against him! Even the servants have turned against him. The bandwagon reads "Down with Haman!" and everyone has hopped on!

Oh how quickly bad news spreads! Beware of this! What do we call this passing along of idle talk? Gossip! Look at the list in which Peter includes gossips or busybodies:

> *"But let none of you suffer*
> *as a **murderer**, or as a **thief**,*
> *or as an **evildoer**,*
> *or as a* _____ *in other men's matters."*
> 1 Peter 4:15

We've all heard preaching on gossip, but do we stop and realize how harmful it really is? We may "murder" someone's character, or "steal" their reputation and it certainly is evil! Why are we so anxious to share bad news anyway? If only we could live 1 Corinthians thirteen!

Let's list all that love or charity is or does:

1 Corinthians 13: LOVE IS...

Verse 4:

1. _____
2. _____
3. _____
4. _____
5. _____

Verse 5:

6. _____
7. _____
8. _____
9. _____

Verse 6:

10. _____
11. _____

Verse 7:

12. _____
13. _____
14. _____
15. _____

Verse 8:

16. _____

A good exercise to use with this wonderful love chapter is to put your name in the place of charity.

Wanda suffereth long, Wanda envieth not... That puts things into perspective!

Chapter seven ends with Haman being hung on the very gallows that he prepared for Mordecai; but it doesn't end there.

> *"The ten **sons** of Haman the son*
> *of Hammedatha, the enemy of the Jews, slew they;"*

Here is a warning for us! We all know Numbers 32:23:*"Be sure you sins will find _____ out",* and we expect the *"finding out"* to be a judgment upon us alone. When Haman was conniving to advance himself, he would have said that he was doing it for his sons as well. His advancement would be their advancement, and rightly so. But anything done in an ungodly way will come back to bite you; and unfortunately, it may bite our loved ones as well! Haman's root of bitterness not only defiled him and others, but cost him the life of his sons!

> *"Looking _____ lest any man fail*
> *of the grace of God;*
> *lest any root of bitterness*
> *springing up _____ you,*
> *and thereby _____ be defiled; "*
> Hebrews 12: 15

APPLICATION:
SHARPENING MY TESTIMONY

Do you have a bitter root? ...a bad habit root? ....a lazy root? ...a weak root? What is keeping you from being all that God wants you to be? Is it *"troubling"* you? Will others also be defiled? This can be a serious problem in our homes.

When our daughter was young, she was showing some bad habits that really frustrated me. Then I realized where she had learned them! They were so engrained into my being that I feared that I could not change! In fact, I tried to blame God—He was responsible for making me this way! It was a struggle, but I realized that if I was to have the loving relationship that I wanted with my girl, and if I was to see her change her bad habits, I needed to change **first**! It was a daily struggle in me, but I praise God that He changed me, and continues to change me as I surrender to His will.

Finish the following statement: "If I could change one thing about me (the "inside" me), it would be _____." Now, what do you have to do to change it? You have already taken the hardest step—admitting that there is a problem!

Step Two: PRAY!

Step Three: Find a verse that you can memorize
              that will help you.

Step Four: Make 20 copies and put them all over
              the house (No, just kidding–this step
              is only for drastic situations! ☺)

Step Five: CHANGE! It may take **years**, but
              change **can** happen. Look at the
              second word of 1 Peter 5:8. That's
              the key! There is instruction,
              admonition, and reason all in that
              one little verse!

Step Six: Stay close to your loving heavenly
              Father.

Chain of Events (chapter eight)

1. Esther gets Haman's _____ (I've often
   wondered what happened to Haman's wife)
   [8:1]
2. Mordecai gets the king's signet ring, and
   Esther sets him over Haman's house [8:2]
3. King Ahasuerus holds out the golden
   scepter yet again to Esther [8:4]
4. The king's letters are reversed (notice
   how often Esther now refers to HER

people in verse six)

5. Mordecai goes out in royal apparel [8:15]
6. Shushan rejoices and is glad [8:15]
7. *"The Jews had light, and gladness, and joy, and honour."* [8:16]
8. *"many of the people of the land* _____ *Jews; for the* _____ *of the Jews fell upon them."* [8:17]

These were good times for the Jewish population. They were a people in a foreign land—carried away as slaves. I'm sure they were disdained by some, just left alone by others. Whatever the case, they remained distinctly different. The culture they brought with them was different: different customs, different dress, different diet and most of all, their religion was different!

Now all has changed. Why? To those living in a faraway province like India, the King and Queen in Shushan were very disconnected from their lives. All the happenings didn't usually affect them. Not too long ago, their young girls were taken from them, never to be seen again—and the law was laid down for women everywhere—obey and respect your husbands or else!

Then the command had come to fight, kill, and destroy the Jews. Some surely ignored it, but to those who were gain-seekers, they had their eyes set on the wealth that the Jews had acquired! They would follow the king's command to destroy all Jews and keep the spoils.

Now this! Surprise, surprise! The queen is a Jew; and the Jews were given the authority to fight back! No easy snatch of treasure now! Why did some decide to become Jews? Surely some did it to find favor in the authority's eye. But others saw something different: the Jews had something they want–a God that sees and hears!

The Jews had remained steadfast to their God throughout all their trials and misery! The Jews had victory over their enemies. Here is an interesting note: What similar phrase do you see in chapter 9, verses 10, 15, and 16?

_____

Integrity–the standard with which they ruled themselves–would not allow them to take of the spoils or kill the women and children, as it had been designed against them! It also showed the people of the land that the Jews desired only to glorify their God, not snatch up the worldly possessions of their enemies. THAT was appealing to the Medes and

Persians who had conquered all, but were left empty-hearted!

We are surrounded by people just like the Medes and Persians. They are grasping for gold and left empty. What do we show forth to the unsaved world around us? Do we show a peace that can only come from God, or are we as miserable and complaining as they are?

Certainly the Jews now shouted for joy and gladness. But for folks to had been converted, they must have shown forth something more! Inner peace–the world is dying for it!

A reason **is** given for the conversions:

"for the _____ of the Jews fell upon them."
[9:17]

Why fear? Because the impossible had happened. Certainly, the God of the Jews must be powerful to be able to orchestrate such a change!

And to think, all these blessings came because one girl sacrificed her life's dreams, was obedient to the will of God, and did the extraordinary. How many were blessed? We have no idea. How many would be blessed if you or I did the same?

Remember:

All the drama is over. Life has settled down. The feasting is over. What's next?

We've had moments like that, after a big event or even a holiday. Life goes on, and we forget all that the Lord has done for us. Mordecai was so set on not letting the people forget what God had done, that the Feast of Purim was established—celebrated on the days that Haman had chosen with the lot to destroy them!

Do we forget what God has done for us? When you need to remember something, what do you do?_____ I am not a very good example of someone who always remembers, but my husband is. His best attack against forgetting is to write it down. Our son uses his cell phone which has an alarm on it. He can set it days in advance. For example, he would often forget to take the trash out, so he would set his alarm to go off to remind him! I often turn my ring around if I just need to remember something for a short time; however, lately the little gray cells are losing their memory power, and I need to do something more concrete to remember!

Whatever your method, could it be used to remember what God has done for us? We could write down his blessings, which we've already done in lesson five! Having scripture on the walls of our homes will help us remember the promises of God. Perhaps doing a word study in the Bible on "remember" or "forget not" would be a great help AND blessing; because, even though we may forget God, He never forgets us!

Get the Word out!

Queen Esther and Mordecai had quite an important message to get out to the people. We see that they made every effort to make sure the message got through.

"And he wrote in the king Ahasuerus' name,
and _____ it with the king's ring,
and sent letters by posts on horseback,
and riders on mules, camels,
and young dromedaries:" [8:10]

1. It was sealed with the king's ring. So is our message! God's Word of salvation, as well as all the promises of God, is sealed by the King of Kings. We need not worry that it is not genuine or lacks power.

*"For ever, O LORD, thy word is **settled** in heaven."*
Psalm 119:89

"For verily I say unto you,
Till heaven and earth pass,
one jot or one tittle shall in no wise pass
from the law,
*till **all** be fulfilled."*
Matt. 5: 18

2. It was in every _____ *"after their language, and to the Jew according to their writing, and according to their language."* [8:9b]
3. It was sent to _____ province [8:9]
4. It was sent with _____ *"So the posts that rode upon mules and camel went out, being hastened and pressed on by the king's commandment. And the decree was given at Shushan the palace."* [8:14]

So, our final lesson from Esther is this: How well are we doing at getting the Gospel out to our lost and dying world? It's a never ending battle to keep the flag flying high! It's a battle we need to keep before us EVERY day. It's easy to be like the Israelites and forget. You may think, "We are God's chosen people; we are safe and secure—and they're not listening anyway!" **We can't do that.**

"Let your light so _____ before men,
that they may _____ your good works,
and _____ your Father which is in heaven."
Matthew 5:16

Esther, the star!

Her true riches started from within
and shone out to her world,
saved and unsaved alike.
Her "calling" was of national importance,
but in God's eyes,
your little corner is just as important!

Shine for Jesus!

One taper lights a thousand,
yet shines as it has shone;
and the humblest light
may kindle one brighter than its own.
-Butterworth